ELLIOTT BURNS

FROM RELIGION TO CONSCIOUSNESS

ELLIOTT BURNS
Edited by Keith Thomas Walker

KEITHWALKERBOOKS, INC
This is a UMS production

FROM RELIGION TO CONSCIOUSNESS

KEITHWALKERBOOKS

Publishing Company
KeithWalkerBooks, Inc.
P.O. Box 331585
Fort Worth, TX 76163

All rights reserved. Except for use in any review, the reproduction or utilization of this manuscript in whole or partial in any form by any mechanical, electronic, or other means, not known or hereafter invented, including photocopying, xerography, and recording, or in any information retrieval or storage system, is forbidden without written permission of the publisher, KeithWalkerBooks, Inc.

For information write
KeithWalkerBooks, Inc.
P.O. Box 331585
Fort Worth, TX 76163

Copyright © 2017 Elliott Burns

ISBN-13 DIGIT: 978-0-9967505-8-5
ISBN-10 DIGIT: 0996750584
Library of Congress Control Number: 2017949630
Manufactured in the United States of America

Second Edition

Visit us at www.keithwalkerbooks.com

ELLIOTT BURNS

ALSO BY ELLIOTT BURNS

Pharisees Behind the Pulpit
(On sale now)

FROM RELIGION TO CONSCIOUSNESS

TABLE OF CONTENTS

Acknowledgments   Page 6

Forward
By Keith Thomas Walker   Page 7

Introduction   Page 10

Chapter 1
What is Consciousness?   Page 17

Chapter 2
Churches or Circuses   Page 23

Chapter 3
Bible Biblas   Page 40

Chapter 4
Christos Hebrews or Coons?   Page 55

Chapter 5
From The Cross To The Ankh   Page 69

Chapter 6
Afrakan Spirituality Science   Page 86

Conclusion   Page 95

ACKNOWLEDGMENTS

First I would like to thank the Supreme Being in the Afrakan trinity Amun, Ptah, Ra or Olodumare, Olorun, Olofi. I would also like to thank my family and community who helped shape my very existence. I'd like to thank my parents who conceived me, kept me, raised me and loved me. Finally, I would like to thank you, the reader, for taking the time and effort to read this book.

FORWARD

Greetings.

Elliott Burns is a friend and coworker I've known for years. I published his first book, *Pharisees Behind the Pulpit*, and was taken aback by his educated attack on modern-day Christian practices. Whether you agree or disagree with the points he makes, you cannot overlook the research that led to his way of thinking.

I had an open mind when Burns approached me again, eager to publish a second book. Hopefully you'll have an open mind as well, because Burns takes his arguments a step further with his latest release. This time he delivers a powerful argument against religion altogether.

Burns believes worshippers, black Americans in particular, should cast off the shackles of "white Jesus" and embrace their ancestral spirituality. We should become *conscious* and understand that all religions have stolen from ancient "Afrakan" spirituality. With lies and "religious books," Christians, Muslims and Hebrews use religion to control the masses.

Did I mention you're going to need an open mind?

I enjoyed working on this book, because knowledge is power. Regardless of whether you or I choose to adopt Burns' teaching into our lives, hopefully you will delve deeper into the information he provides. His arguments are as thought-provoking as they are poignant.

If you're black in America, at some point you may have wondered where you would be, on a spiritual level, if not for the slave trade. If the answer to that question makes you uncomfortable, ask yourself why. If you're interested in exploring the secrets religion has been hiding from you, please continue reading.

KEITH THOMAS WALKER

INTRODUCTION

This book has been on my mind since I wrote my first book, *Pharisees Behind the Pulpit*. My thinking has grown a lot since then, as I've grown in knowledge and wisdom. When I was a Christian, I would listen to my father. He is deceased now, but his soul lives forever. My father had no problem disagreeing with the pastor. The same could be said for my wife, whose soul also lives forever.

The problem is, when you openly disagree with your pastor, you are considered a "bad church member" for having a mind of your own. The uncomfortable situations I've been in have always stayed in the back of my mind.

When I became a pastor of my own congregation, I knew I needed to learn more. As I educated myself and dug into different teachings, I was surprised by all of the lies that were told to me in history class and church. My late wife, who was once a Christian, became conscious as well. Before she passed, one of her requests was for me to wake my people after she transcended. I promised her I would, and that vow led to this book.

Hotep, Shalam, Peace, Ire, my beautiful brothers and sisters. Let me introduce myself. My name is Aliyahu Amun. I have two names; one my parents gave me at birth and a spiritual name given to me at birth by the most high divine. I did not have to change my name. Elliott comes from the Hebrew name *Aliyahu*, and I was born on the day and month of Amen, Amun, Amon, Niyome.

But what's in a name? Actually, there's quite a bit. *Al* means *god*. According to the bible, *Yahu* (or Yahua Jehovah) means self-existing, but *Yah* is a kemetic, kamitic, Egyptian word that means "moon deity" or "neteru nature."

Al, Alahim, Elohim or El was originally a Sumerian deity of the sky. Amun also was a kamitic name meaning "hidden," which is another name for the Supreme Being. And the word God, or *Gawd*, is another Hebrew name for a deity meaning "fortune luck." In Kamit, the word God is "*Gawga*," which means "loud noise crackling, pour into." This is "the big bang" Amun used to start the creation process.

You can understand how "*pour into*" became "*fortune luck*." Even today people still say, "God poured into my life." You can see how just in the etymology of my name alone proves the bible is not monotheistic (the worship of one god). Instead it's *polytheistic*; which is the worship of many Afrakan gods that look like one god. The trinity is proof of that.

Many people don't agree with that. They would rather call Egyptian spirituality *voodoo*. They believe *Obeah* and *Ifa* are evil. If that was the case, then Christianity, Islam and Judaism must look in the mirror, because their religious ideas came from Afraka.

The purpose of this book is to open up your other sleeping conscious, or as some call it, your *third eye*. This book does talk about religion. Why? Because when you break down the word, *religion* means (re) "regather" (ligion) "many." Religion is supposed to help us regather many ideas to bring everyone back to one source, or god. But the problem is the word is not used that way.

If you look up the definition of "religion," you'll learn that it means to practice a certain culture's spiritual attitudes or beliefs. This why when you change from one religion to another (like Christian, European culture to Islamic culture), you *convert*. True spirituality does not call for such nonsense as a conversion. You're born with a unique, spirit energy, but you're *taught* religion.

Some of you reading this are double conscious. For examplc, most of us use the term *African-American*. You're born in American culture, but your conscious is aware that you are African. The problem with this is there are some of us who are not aware of our Afrakan culture, because of the religion you choose to practice. You put Christmas before Kwanzaa.

So why is this a problem? Here's a reality check: Praying to foreign (European gods) has done nothing for our people. I will reveal why later. It's time to drop religion altogether and become *conscious*. I am not a master teacher, but if I give you enough food for thought, my hope is that you will get hungry for more *soul food* (spiritual teaching).

CHAPTER ONE
WHAT IS CONSCIOUSNESS?

The problem with the words *conscious* and *conscious community* is they're being misused by some, the same way the word *religion* misleads some people. Case in point, there is no such thing as a singular conscious community. "Commonplace common interest" it is not a religion, because each group may not practice spirituality the same way. One may do yoga, while others prefer libation. *Conscious* simply means "aware, awake," but your awareness is dependent on what you learned. Everyone is on a different conscious level or subject.

People ask me all the time, "What's your religion?" I respond, "Conscious." That is not what I practice, because consciousness is not a religion. I practice *Ifa life* and *KaMa'at soul balance*. I don't believe the bible is a book of facts. Instead, it has misleading stories as well as some good moral stories and proverbs.

I will use one to make a point: The bible says, "*For as a man thinks in his heart, so is he.*" I could care less what you call yourself, however your beliefs, religion and state of mind will always determine your actions. If you're a Muslim, for example, you don't eat pork. If you discover the people in the bible are black, you might practice Judaism, which I think is a mistake, but I will deal with that later.

If you think the Jews are God's "chosen white people," and Jesus is also white, then you may have problems with your own race. Most people associate consciousness with not believing in religion, which for the most part is correct. When you become conscious, you become aware of religious lies.

I will use another bible verse to make a point: *"Be ready always to give an answer to every man that asks you a reason of the hope that is in you."*

While that does apply to believers, it also applies to conscious people, even though we do not go around knocking on people's doors trying to convert them.

If someone asks you, "What is consciousness, and why are you conscious?" you should be able to give an answer. Knowing that your answer will not be a religious one, you should not waste your time arguing with people on social media about what consciousness is and what it is not, and what conscious people should believe and how they should practice.

Spending a lot of time on YouTube does not make you conscious. I am grateful for those who read books, because books can make you aware of the lies and truths, if you find the right authors. But knowing yourself and self-awareness cannot come solely from a book.

There is an Egyptian proverb that says, *"The body is the house of God."* That is why it's important to know yourself. Another Egyptian proverb says, *"The kingdom of heaven is within you, and whosoever shall know himself shall find it."*

Consciousness is a double-edged sword. While conscious people are not religious, we become aware of who we are, who our ancestors are and how our behavior has changed with dignity. While you may be angry at first when you uncover all the European lies and how your true ancestral history was hidden from you, true conscious people do not lash out on social media or stand on street corners cursing at white people.

CHAPTER TWO
CHURCHES OR CIRCUSES

Consider these teachings my notes from studying with a Christian mindset, so you can see how I woke up. Now, I showed you who God really is (fortune luck). When we pray to the Christian *God*, what do think it does to you? The proof is in the churches themselves.

Think of the tithes and offerings; how the collection plate is passed three times because the pastor needs a raise or to bulk up the building fund. Think of how prosperity churches have an endless list of how much money they need. They always need more money, more money and then some more money.

Now ask yourself, if all of your resources are going to these churches, who is giving money back to our communities? Before you say, "My church gives back to the community," do a reality check. In every hood, there is a liquor store, a loan company and a church on every corner. Are all communities like this?

If you ask a Muslim how many mosques there are in his city, most of them will be able to count them on one hand. Remember, I was a pastor. I know the hustle. When the bidding starts during offering, the pastor is lying when he says the Holy Spirit told him, "There is $50 on this side of the building." What he's really doing is looking at the most well dressed people on that side.

The tithes are supposed to belong to the community, not the church, if you believe the bible. Also the tithes do not refer to money in the bible (*Deuteronomy 14:29*, *Deuteronomy 26:12*, *Malachi 3:5*, *James 1:27*, *Luke 11:42*, *Matthew 23:23*). But that's only if you're going by the bible. There is nothing wrong with tithes, if they are given back to the proper source. But these days our money is divided, because our churches are divided. We do not need a church on every corner.

The biggest hustle is when you hear someone say, "I am Dr. John Doe. I went to seminary, so I know more than the next preacher." By the time you finish this book, you will understand that people like John really know little to nothing. I don't mean that as an insult. But the truth is going to seminary is like letting your enemy prepare your meals. For example, if you want to kill an ant hill, you feed the poison to the foot soldiers. The soldiers then take the poison to the queen. Once you kill the queen, you kill the ant hill.

Many pastors have been fed poison. They take that poison to the congregation, and black people have been dying ever since. There's an African proverb that states, "If you educate a man, you educate an individual. But if you educate a woman, you educate a nation." This is true because the woman is the teacher of the children. If you poison the mind of the woman, you destroy a whole nation. Unfortunately, no one loves to white wash Jesus more than black queens.

Don't get me wrong, if Christianity, Islam or Judaism helps you get through the day, then do you. However, the problem I have is the commandment, "Thou shall not lie." Or how about *Psalms 101:7*, "He that works deceit shall not dwell within my house. He that tells lies shall not remain in my (sight presence)."

John 16:13 says the Holy Spirit is the spirit of truth. But this presents a bigger problem, because no one was born in a manger with the name *Jesus* or *Yeshua*. This miraculous birth could not have taken place on December 25th. Someone got the math wrong, because from Friday to Sunday is not three days and nights, and the Sabbath was never on Sunday. But it's okay to lie, if it's in the name of religion, right? It seems Christians are overlooking the truth in their own bible.

Before the Paul worshipers start quoting him in an attempt to prove me wrong, let's look at *Colossians 2:16*, "Let no man therefore condemn you in meat or drink, or in the respect of (holidays, holydays), or new moon or of the

Sabbath days." In *Colossians 2:8*, Paul warned us to beware of man's calendar rudiments. Paul was not trying to justify Sunday, Christmas or Easter. He was in support of *Appointed Muadim*, which are days found in *Leviticus 23*. *Isaiah 1:14* says, "Your new moons and your appointed feast my soul hates. They are a trouble unto me. I am disgusted to bear them."

    This chapter is not to bash religion or uncover every lie, because that would take about 100 books worth of information. Instead, this chapter is to get you to see and filter out European culture in your religion. For example, have you ever asked yourself why Jesus is pictured in a white, Greek Roman robe with long brown hair and blue eyes? That should have been the first light bulb that went off in your head.

Here's another question: Why are angels depicted as European with wings? And why are the names in the bible Greek? Before the King James version of the bible, no one called on angels, Jesus, a Holy Spirit or Jehovah. Now, while I do believe the Supreme Being manifests itself through different attributes or names in every religion, each name calls for a different vibration (or energy). This why I said the bible is not monotheistic, because the names in the bible are not translations.

For example, Jehovah is not a translation of Yahuah. "Je" is for "Jove," a Roman god of Jupiter. "Hovah" means wicked, ruin and disaster. Not only has the letter "J" been around for about 500 years, but "Yeshua" is incorrect as well. "Ye" is Yiddish. "Shua" means "cry for help." So Jesus' name could not have been "Yahshua," because that means, "Yah cries for help." Neither "Jesus" nor "Yeshua" means salvation. Nor does Immanuel, but I will deal with that later.

    If you do the research, you'll see that "*angels*" is just another term for Anglo Saxons. *Holy* is just another name for the deity of the sun. I know the vibrations of Amun and Yah, because I know what their names mean. So why would I call Greek Roman gods to my aid once I know better? Even if Allah and Yah are both moon gods, Muslims do not call on Yah, and

Hebrews do not call on Allah, because of cultural differences. Switching names would bring a different *vibration feel* or *energy mood* to their temples.

Even though I know Satanism got the Baphomet from the Kamatic goat of Mendez, I still will not call on the Baphomet, because it is still a satanic god. I would not call on Lucifer either, even though the name only means "light bringer," because it is still a Luciferian god.

When translated correctly, Jesus refers to Lucifer as "the bright morning star," *2 Peter 1:19, Revelation 22:16*. Jesus and Lucifer are enemies in the Christian mind, so to call the Latin name "Jesus" by his other Latin name "Lucifer" is a no-no.

So why do Afakans call on their enemy's god? Instead they should, "Throw away the symbol of the god of the whites, who so often caused us to weep, and listen to the voice of liberty," (*Boukman Haitian revolt, August 22, 1791*). So I ask you, why do you have the image of a white man on your wall? In the Roman catacombs, the images of Jesus and Hebrews are black.

The Roman historian Tacitus wrote this about Hebrews: "Many again say they were a race of Ethiopian origin." So why is there an image of a white man on the shroud of Turin, when the oldest images of Jesus and his mother depict them as black?

The shroud of Turin, on more than one occasion, has been called a fake, in spite what some scientists claim. First of all, many still dispute its proper date. I believe Jesus had two facelifts; one from Serapes, a half Greek, half Egyptian god created to trick the Afrakans into worshipping it. The other facelift is Borgia Cesar. I believe this is the face on the shroud of Turin.

The *Wisdom of Solomon 14:15* states, "For a father afflicted with untimely mourning, when he hath made an image of his child soon taken away, now honored him as god, which was then a dead man, and delivered to those that were under him ceremonies and sacrifices."

Now you might be thinking I am being harsh by using the word "circus" in this chapter title. The reason I used it is because the word "church" literally means "circus." The word "church" does not come from the Greek word "ecclesia." "Ecclesia" means assembly, congregation. The word church comes from Circe, the Greek goddess of animals. She is sometimes pictured with a cup of spells in her hand. "Circe" was later translated to "circus."

Now read *Revelation 17: 4-5*:
"And the woman was dressed in purple and red color, {Catholic colors} and decked with gold and expensive stones and pearls, having a golden cup in her hand full of (idols, taboo) and filthiness of her harlotry. And upon her head was a name written, mystery (Babil Gate) the

mother of harlots and (idols, taboo) of the earth."

Someone (not John) went through a lot of trouble to let people know the church is misleading the world. Not only did they use the word *church* (Circe), but they used the Catholic colors and the word "mother" before Babil Gate.

The Strong's Concordance has been known to mislead people as well. For example, the word "Babylon" does not mean confusion. They're telling people that Catholicism is the gateway, the mother of taboo practices, in all denominations.

There are many denominations of one religion. This why I don't use (re) gather (legion) many, because

Catholicism is the false mother of spiritual practices. Afraka is the real mother of spiritual practices.

CHAPTER THREE
BIBLE BIBLAS

"When the missionaries came to Africa, they had the Bible and we had the land. They said, 'Let us pray.' We closed our eyes. When we opened them, we had the Bible, and they had the land" (Desmond Tutu).

The bible originally was called *bibla* in Latin, or *Byblos*. Byblos was also an Egyptian goddess of paper (papyrus). The problem with the bible is it is not a translation but a *transliteration*. This why a concordance is needed to interpret it, rather than a regular dictionary. To put it simply, the bible has *replacement words* in it, not *translated words*. So how can this be the word of God, if it's full of lies?

For instance, the word "Jew" is not a translation. Someone just put the word in the bible. Judaism is not a B.C.E. (before common error) religion, but a C.E. (common error) religion. In other words, Judaism is a medieval religion. There is also no prophecy of Jesus being called Immanuel. That means there are flat out lies in the bible, not just mistranslations. Even the term "word of God" was stolen from Afrakans. The phrase is Egyptian. It was called

"Meter Neter," which means "divine speech."

Again, I am not trying to convert anyone. While the bible is not a book of actual events and facts, it's still a book of moral stories. People often defend the bible by referring to the prophecies that came to pass, but I have a question: Came to pass is determined by whom?

If we take an ink blot picture, and five people look at it, each person may see something different. Now let us look at the book of Revelation. Some will say they saw blood lakes, but the red lakes did not have actual blood in them. Some even say between 2010 and 2013, they heard a trumpet blast coming from the sky. But the bible said Jesus is going to appear during the trump blast. So where is he?

How can the Old Testament be the prophecy of Jesus, when no one can even prove he existed? People will tell you the prophecy said Jerusalem will become a nation again. The key word is "again." I don't see the original Afrakan Hebrews ruling Jerusalem. So how can a prophecy be a prophecy if the people who wrote it lived after the event?

The gospel was not written until years after Jesus and his disciples supposedly died. Back then, no one used the English names Matthew, Mark, Luke and John. Here is another fact: The events in the bible do not match real time events in history, which reminds me, where are the dates in the bible? Surprise, they are not there.

When I was a young preacher, every vacant lot I saw, I envisioned a church being built there. Now that I am awake, I would rather see community centers being built on those vacant lots. We need to change the way we think and the way we view things.

Now, I promised I would finish what I started in the previous chapter about Jesus' name and Immanuel. The word "Jesus" should not even be in the bible. "*Yeshua*" and "*Yahshua*" are supposed to be "Joshua" in English. But it's more complicated than that, because each time you see "Joshua" in the bible, it is actually a different name in Hebrew. There is "Joshua HushaYa." There is

"Joshua Yeshua." There is "Joshua Yahushua," and there is "Joshua Yahusha." I am only going to focus on two of these names; *Joshua Yahusha* and *Joshua HushaYa*.

You may have noticed at the beginning of the book I said *Aliyahu* is "thought to be Hebrew." I said this because a lot of ancient Egyptian words were passed off as Hebrew. For example, Moses Joshua, son of Nun, is "HushaYa" in Hebrew. Once again, this is a Hebrew god.

Yahuah was the Egyptian moon god. If you drop the "a" from Yah shua, you'll have "Shu," which is the Egyptian god of air. Nun is the Egyptian god of the black universe, primeval waters. In other words, they were calling black space black waters.

Even the name *Moses* was Egyptian in nature, derived from "Thotmos." Remember, Moses was named by an Egyptian, not a Hebrew *Exodus 2:10*. "Draw out" in Hebrew is *Mashah*. In biblical prophecy, Jesus' name was *Yahusha*, named after Joshua the high priest, *Zechariah 3:8* and *Zechariah 6:12*.

Yahusha means "Yahuah saves," *Matthew 1:23*. *Immanuel* does not mean "God is with us." That is flat out another lie. Emmanual is supposed to be Hebrew (*Ammanual*). It means "God is with men," or with a "multitude of men," because the prophecy was not about Jesus. It was about Hezekiah Isaiah.

"Therefore the Lord himself shall give you a sign, behold a young (maiden almah) shall conceive, and bear a son, and shall call his name Ammanual." The word virgin was put there later. The correct translation is *maiden*. When you have some time, read *2 Chronicles 32:8, Isaiah 8:8, Isaiah 7:16-17, Isaiah 8:1-4, 2 Chronicles 30:2-3, Isaiah 9:7, Isaiah 39:8, 2 Chronicles 29:2* and *31:20*. All of these passages will explain how Hezekiah is not Jesus.

But the problem with Hezekiah's prophecy is *Ammanual* is not even Hebrew. Technically, it means "Amman Amen is God." Jesus, out of his own mouth, confirms this in *Revelation 3:14*:

"These things said the Amen, the faithful and true witness, the beginning of the creation of Alahim." Notice when you use the Hebrew *Alahim* instead of the Greek Theo's for God, it changes the whole verse.

Remember, Jesus spoke Hebrew in the bible, *Matthew 27:46, Acts 26: 14-15*. Now remember "El Al" is singular, and "Elohim Alahim" is plural. Now let's use the correct translation of *Revelation 3:14*, "These things said Amun, the faithful and true witness, the beginning of creation of gods." Anyone who studies ancient Egyptian will see this a mile away *Deuteronomy 6:4*, "Hear Shema O Israel the Lord our God is one."

Remember monotheism started in Egypt first. Through Amun came other "neterus, nature" form of himself in what we call *deities*, but these are not different gods, when using the correct form of thought.

"Shema" in Hebrew means *obey*. But the problem again is this is an Egyptian word; "*sema*," which means "yoke, yoga." This word is also pronounced *smaitwai*. That means this whole verse is Egyptian. Yoga refers to tying your lower self to your higher self or divine conscious by using *sema*.

The word *Israel* was also originally Egyptian. It was called *Sharma*, which means "peace, content."

Later it was changed to "shalam, shalom."

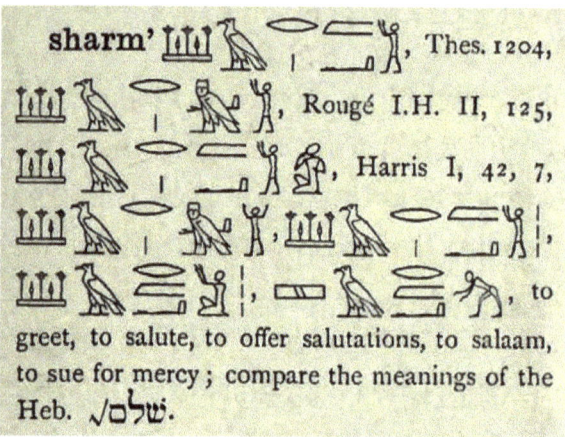

The word *Lord* in Hebrew is *Adonia*. The "ia" is Yiddish, so it was pronounced *Adon, Adon*, which comes from "Aton, Aten." The *d* was replaced with a *t*. The word *Ra* in Hebrew means *evil*, but why? It is because Akhenaton changed *Ra* from being the sole deity to *Aton*?

Now let's look at *Deuteronomy 6:4*. Again "Shema O sharma the Aton our Alahim Neterus is one." Like I said, the whole verse is Egyptian. The Hebrews called themselves *Yahudi*. But remember, the *d* has replaced a *t*. "Yahuti" is the Egyptian moon deity *Iah Yah*. *Hosea 13:4* says, "Yet I am the Lord your God from the land of Egypt." In fact, the Kabbalah is a stolen version of the Egyptian tree of life, but the Jews will tell you it means *teachings*.

The truth is the word *Kabbala* is Egyptian as well. "Ka" means soul, "ba" means heart, and "La" means Yah. Together they mean "Yah heart and soul." I know for a fact *Ezekiel 10:14* never happened. This is because the Sphinx, which was originally called "Haru on two horizons," is where they got the ideal of the cherubim's "lion fall," "bull summer," "eagle winter," and "man spring." Khnum was seen at the potter's wheel first creating man *Jeremiah 18:1-6, Isaiah 64:8*.

The name *Abraham* is also in question. It's supposed to mean "father prince of many nations." But the correct spelling for that would be *Abrahim*. So let's examine the name Abraham according to the bible. We know that *ham* was used to describe black people. I believe this was a slick way of saying *kam* from *kamit,* meaning "black community." This was later called Egypt, meaning "temple soul of Ptah."

Abraham means "black father, prince of multitude." But this name can also be kamitic, in which case it means "black Ra spirit." The Star of David is just two pyramids put together.

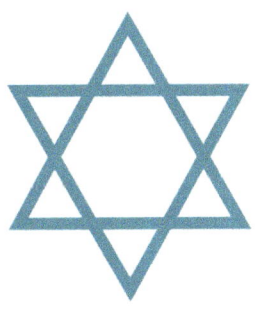

The word *Christ* comes from "Krishna," an Indian deity. The word *Messiah* comes from "*messah*," a kamitic word that means anointed. As you can see, the bible was kamitic in nature.

"White man speak with a fork tongue," (*Native American Proverb*).

After reading the last two chapters, who can argue with that truth?

CHAPTER FOUR
CHRISTOS HEBREWS OR COONS?

Please don't be offended by the title of this chapter. I am not trying to pick a fight with the black Hebrews. In fact, I converted from Christianity to Black Hebrew Israelite also, like most in the secret name movement, before I became conscious.

But there are some black people who have allowed the bible to turn them into coons. Black Hebrews and Christians are alike. People say we lost our spiritual practice during slavery. This is not true. We just *forgot* our spiritual practice, because when reading bible stories to our children (for those who could read), we forgot to tell them they were not real events but moral points. Also we could not read them our own stories; showing them how we hid our spiritual practices in modern Christianity.

    Christianity came before Islam and Judaism. The Greeks and Romans stole it from us and changed it to fit their culture. They then used it to rule people. We did not use the word *Christian*. That word comes from the Latin word "*certin*," which means "idiot, retard." "Those who worship Serapes are Christians, and those who call themselves bishops of Christ are devoted to Serapes," *Hadrian to Servianus, 134 B.C.E.*

The word "Christian" only appears in the bible three times, and each time no one called themselves "Christians," *Acts 11:26, Acts 26:28* and *1 Peter 4:16*. Serapes' title was *christus*, which means "anointed healer." But just like the word "negus" (niggas) and "rulers" (gods), it became a slur thanks to racism.

The Greek New Testament did not have the word *cross* in it, but it had the words *stake*, *impale* and *tree*. Again, the word *cross* was not a translation. It was simply put in the bible. The cross came from the *ankh*. "The ancient

Egyptian hieroglyphic symbol of life - the ankh, a tau cross surmounted by a loop and known as crux ansata - was adopted and extensively used on Coptic Christian monuments," *The New Encyclopedia Britannica 1995*.

The word *Coptic* means *Ethiopian*. There are no crosses on the Constantine monument, which means Constantine lied about his vision of the cross. Besides, the Hebrew tau and Constantine cross are shaped like an *x*, not a *t*. Later the shape of the tau was changed.

The ankh means "breath of life." Sound familiar (*Genesis 2:7*)? The ankh represents life both in the physical plane and spiritual plane. It is a vagina and a penis put together. The vagina is the gateway between the spiritual realm and the physical realm. Some call the cross "the cross roads," which sounds familiar, if you practice voodoo. Again, it represents both the physical plane and spiritual plane in life and death.

When slaves were brought to the United States to Jamestown (which was named after King James), they traveled on the "Good Ship of Jesus." Later the Copts in James Town built a Baptist church. In it you will find they hid their spiritual practices in modern Christianity. The top half of the church was white. The bottom half was red. This, of course, mirrors the crown of kamit.

The church was also used for the underground runaway slaves. In the floor, you can see the markings of what looks like a Kongo cross, which also represents the life and death crossroads of Ra and Khepra. You see, we still held onto our spiritual practices. We just hid them.

If *voodoo*, *Vodun Spirit* and *Ifa Life* are evil in the Hebrew and Christian minds, then why does the God of the bible approve it under a different name? *Urim* and *Thummim* means, "light and perfection." You also may know it as "casting lots," *Exodus 28:30, Ezra 2:63, Nehemiah 7:65, Numbers 26:55, Acts 1:26.*

Remember, the first mention of a bible was in kamit, but it was destroyed by fire, allowing other people to change it, or better yet, write a new one. "And laid open the book of the law, wherein the heathen had sought to paint the likeness of their images," *1 Maccabees 3:48*. This happened in the land we call Jerusalem and other places as well.

    While I learned a lot under the title "black Israelite," I also found myself picking up bad information from them, like the lie that the Afrakans gave us to the white man because we were Hebrews, or the lie that "Afrakan Egyptians" are our enemies, which leads to division amongst ourselves. Or how about the Christians who thank God for slavery, because without it they would be in Afraka practicing voodoo, never knowing Jesus could forgive all of their sins?

FROM RELIGION TO CONSCIOUSNESS

This is the type of thinking that can develop when you believe the bible is 100% factual. You learn to hate your own culture and accept European lies. One day, out of the blue, "The Lord of the cosmos" put a question in my conscious: If Christians and black Hebrews got their customs from Afraka, then why are we calling the Afrakan practices pagan?

Then I asked myself, if monotheism came from kamit, then how is the story of Moses true? You see, if the "Holy of Holy's," baptism, anointing and circumcision started in kamit, then how can we fix our mouths to call Afrakan culture pagan? Where I'm from, that is called *house Negro buffoonery*! It doesn't matter what you call yourself (black Israelite, Muslim, Christian, Ifa, Moore), it all means nothing if we can't walk in black unity.

While the black Hebrews do recognize that Joseph was Imhotep with an Egyptian bloodline, they neglect the fact that Hebrews were not slaves. They were just one tribe of many in kamit. Black Hebrews do not accept that they bred with other Afrakans, even though it was polygamy that made them grow, *Genesis 46:26-27, Exodus 12:37*. But the bible says different, *Ezekiel 47:22, Exodus 12:37-38*. Some believe the Levites (Luim, Limba) were not Hebrews but Egyptians (kam'au). *Kam'au* means "divine black." This is the real reason they did not receive any inheritance, *Numbers 18:20*.

Whether you believe the bible or not, other races will always consider you *black*, no matter what you call yourself. We have a common problem that needs real solutions, other than keeping the commandments. The problem with any religion its religious book. If you take away the religious book, you take away the argument that their book is from God.

For example, as a Christian preacher, it was pounded in our heads that we should "test the spirit, to see if it is from God." How do you test the spirit? For one, the prophet must produce good works. Secondly, you have to determine if the prophet's prophecies came to past. Third, you have to determine if his spirit lines up with the word.

Now let's test the word itself. If the prophecies in the book do not come to pass nor do they line up with actual events, how can that book be from God? Take away the book, and you take away religious arguments. Black Hebrew Israelites argue that the curses in the bible only apply to black people, even though the bible was changed more times than anyone can count.

I will agree that many of the curses in the bible do apply to black people, however, if you ask a Black Hebrew to confirm the bible with DNA testing, their prophecy of the twelve tribes will fall apart. They believe the tribe of Juda represents America, but the truth is no one knows what tribe they came from. If their DNA reveals they are from a tribe they believe is pagan, how embarrassing would that be?

Another thing to note is that if you are in a particular country due to the Atlantic slave trade, then you are not pure anything. You are Afrakan by birth, but you have a choice of which religion you choose.

Let us put the bible through another test: Was there really a great Exodus, and did Moses exist? Did the creation story really happen the way the bible says it did? If you take away the foundation, the house of lies will fall. The problem with the story of Moses is a baby floating down the river in a basket is a Sumerian story that existed long before any one named Moses came along. The story of the great flood was Sumerian as well. The story of a great sea being separated was an Egyptian story that had nothing to do with Moses.

After reading the Sumerian and Egyptian stories of creation, it is easy to see where the bible's story of creation came from. This is why there are two different creation stories in Genesis. The trees in the Garden of Eden (the Tree of Life and the Tree of Knowledge of Good and Evil) were created by a man named Bishop Hippo. Think about it. If God planted the Tree of Knowledge knowing what the outcome would be, wouldn't that make God evil?

The truth is the Exodus never happened. The Roman Tacitcus spilled the beans when he wrote about how the Hebrews were a group of Ethiopians who were exiled due to leprosy. It's easy to prove the people in the bible are Afrakans, but the events in the bible are a problem, so let's put away the events for now and put our minds together for a real time solution to our problems.

CHAPTER FIVE
FROM THE CROSS TO THE ANKH

While the bible is still a good moral book, to believe it literally can turn some people into slaves. I know this because I was one of them. You can become a hostage to what you read. For example, those brainwashed by Christianity can't have pictures and statues of demons and angels. They can't own Afrakan masks or statues.

They can't gamble. They can't watch an R-rated movie. They can't eat this or that. They can't dress like this or that. They can't even get involved with yoga, because the bible says it's demonic. If you're a woman, it's a sin for you to wear pants. The list is endless.

At one point I realized I can't even leave the house without being afraid that I was going to commit a sin. Hell, you can't even go to church without sinning, because if you wear makeup, you've sinned. If you shout, you sin. You'd better say Amen when the preacher is preaching! If you play music in church, you sin. If you don't play music, you sin. And you'd better speak in tongue, or you're a sinner!

And then there's the "Jesus saves" myth. If Jesus saves, he's doing a piss poor job at it for Afrakan people. What woke me up was the secret name movement, *Romans 10:9-10*. How can calling His name save you when no one knows what his correct name is? Is it *Jesus, Joshua, Yeshua, Yahushua, Yahshua* or *Yahusha*. Hell, they can't even get God's name right. Is it *Yahweh, Ha Shem, Yahova, Yehova, Jehova, Ahaya, Ahashiya* or *Yahuah*? You get tongue twisted just trying to say them all.

The point I'm making, before anyone gets in their feelings, is the statement I made earlier in this book. The same picture, different views. The same book, different views, which means something is wrong, if everyone keeps coming up with different translations for the bible. I don't care what translation you use when reading **this** book, because at the end of the day, everyone will have the same meaning.

Now think about religion. I know what the word is thought to mean, but let's be honest, religion has kept the world separated. There have been more wars declared in the name of religion than any other cause. Modern day religion was created for one reason and one reason only: to control a large population in the name of a cultural god.

This is why I left religion. Afrakans never had religion in the first place. You prayed to the name of your choice. As long as we made getting along a top priority, we did not need a book or a preacher screaming at us every Sunday to tell us what was morally right and how to get along with each other.

Do bears, birds, ants and whales need a book to teach them how to be what they are? No, nor do humans. This is the real key to the hieroglyphs. The Lord of the universe, "word of God," is in your DNA. Nature (Neteru) is all around you to help guide you if you tune in. But you can't tune in, because if a preacher is always in your ear, you can't hear what the Lord of the cosmos is trying to tell you.

This is where religion contradicts itself. If we both have the same Holy Spirit, then the Spirit will speak to me about my issues before he will you.

Now, if a person is a sinner and is in moral conflict with themselves, then they will need guidance. But even then Afrakan prophecy works differently than in religion.

While prophecy does mean "to speak the mind of God," a shama does not tell your future. Why? Because the Supreme Being does not take away free will. He will tell you your options, both good and bad, but the choice is yours to do as you will.

To keep this chapter from being too long, let me list all of my reasons for leaving religion for Afrakan spirituality: One, a lie is a lie. I don't care if the lie is meant for good, in the end, it will always produce bad fruit. European Christian culture does not work for Afrakans.

Kam'au (divine black) sounds evil, but what they fail to teach you is scientific facts that prove we are different. Ask yourself why schools and churches do not teach you about the differences between people with melanin and those without. What are they afraid of?

Kamit teaches us that "man was created from the tears (essence matter melanin substance) of Amun." Proof of this is melanin is the same substance that is found in the black universe. Science proved this is in fact true. The lies about our future that are told in school is another reason why European culture is not good for us.

Afraka was not named after Scipio Africanus, but he took on that name after he won the battle against Hannibal.

The word "Au Ra Ka" dates back to kamit, meaning "divine Ra soul." But it later became *Afuraka*, meaning "home of land of the soul."

The main reason I don't follow Christianity is because everything in the bible came from us. You see this both in religion and history. For example, the image of the cherubim on the ark and the ten commands clearly came from kamit. Why would I learn to be moral from the most unjust group on earth in history? Even *Ma'at* (truth, justice, balance, law and order) came from us.

How can you teach me about God, when I was the one who gave you God first? The beautiful thing about Afrakan spirituality is it differs in language, but the practices are the same. This is how the different tribes got along so well in kamit.

Ifa is just as old, if not older, than kamit. But the point is, nothing changed in its practices. This goes back to the point I made earlier: I could care less what name you choose to call the divine, as long as our practices keep us in harmony.

Afrakan spirituality is meant to strengthen your soul, not give you conflicting laws. For example, the 42 Philosophy's of Ma'at are not commandments. They are meant to build character. The Lord of the cosmos evaluates the heart and does not condemn you to hell if you break a rule. Laws are flawed because they can't fit every situation. What good is a command if it does not build character?

You don't need a list of commandments about how to treat your wife. Each woman is different. What works for one does not necessarily work for another. The same goes for each person you meet. You don't need a commandment if you know how to reason. You give animals and pets commands, not humans.

Think out the box with me. What people call heaven has no commandments. Why? Because no one is sinning in heaven. The bible says, "Let your will be done on earth as in heaven," "as above so below." Your spiritual practice is to make you divine and Christ-like. Some will say, "You let a dog off its leash, once it learns how to behave." If all of these religions really worked, then why are there so many leashes (commands)?

Don't get me wrong, all religions are to get you closer to God. The closer you get to God, the belief is you will learn to treat all mankind with love. Again, the problem is religion is being taught, rather than spirituality. This is the reason mankind cannot get along. People are being taught what to think and not *how* to think.

I saved the point I am about to make for last, because I wanted to give you enough information to research things on your own, rather than just take my word for it. There will always be that one person who will need a divine act to change their mind. Okay. To put it plain, Jesus was not God in the flesh, nor did he die for your sins. The reason why it is so hard for people to see past the "gospel" is because it does not mean "good news." This is yet another bible lie. "Gospel" really means what it sounds like, "God's spells." Christians are literally under a spell.

For example, if something good happens, like a miracle, depending on what religion you are will determine which god gets credit. The universal term for *God* was *Neb-er-Tcher*, which means "Lord of the cosmos," or "Lord of the utter most limits." To put it simple, this means "Lord of all or everything." The original name for Egypt was "*Ta Mari*," which means *beloved land*.

You can worship Jesus all day, every day. I don't care how many countless people died, because they knew Jesus was going to be used to conquer the free world, and that is what happened. Free people became slaves using god's spells.

Religion is political as well. Create a god and put fear in the parents to teach the children to love and worship it. Make it flawless, and then make it speak by writing letters and stories in God's name, and you just took away free will. People will obey the government through the religion without knowing who the real puppet masters are.

Now let us talk about the greatest secrets never told. Why are Christians not told about the 920 years of war it took to make Jesus divine? Why are Christians not told about the "Jesus scrolls," in which Jesus explains that he is not God? Why are Christians not told about James' (Jesus' brother) letter that is older than the Septuagint that explains that Jesus is not God? Why are Christians are not told that the Catholic encyclopedia admits the bible was forged?

Paul was really Simon Magus. There were no eye witnesses of the New Testament acts. They were written almost thirty plus years later. We know this because the places and times are not accurate. And for the ones who only believe the bible, in *Matthew 19:17* Jesus said out of his own mouth, "Why call me good? There is none good but

[God]." In *Matthew 26:39*, Jesus says "not as I will, but as you (Father) will."

In *Matthew 26:36-4*, *John 17:3* and *Mark 24:32-36*, Jesus does not know the time of his return. Only the Father knows. *John 3:16-17* explains, when read properly, that God is the savior, not Jesus, because we are saved *through* Jesus, not *by* Jesus. The Greek word *redeemer* and Hebrew word *redeemer* are different. The Greek word means *savior*. The Hebrews believe a man who marries his brother's widow to have a child for his dead brother is a redeemer.

The bible says no one can die for your sins, *Deuteronomy 24:16*. Then there is *Psalms 44:21*: If God judges the heart, then why would he send someone to die for your actions? At the council of Nicea, the Christian creed was created: "Virgin birth, trinity, baptism." The problem with this is no one used the word *trinity*. The word used was *Homoousios*, and it does not mean three gods that make one. It means "one substance, or one essence, or one matter."

For example, Hercules is Zeus' son, so Hercules is made up of the same substance as his father, just like angels are made up of the same matter as God, which is spirit. So if that makes Jesus God, then we are all gods, according to the bible. *Genesis 1:26* says, "And God said, let us make man in our image, after our likeness." *Genesis 2:7* says, "And the Lord God formed man of the dust of the ground, and breathed (DNA) into his nostrils."

Remember the ink splash "us" may mean trinity to you but something else to a different person, like angels are deities. Then there is the question of miracles in Jesus' name. But what about miracles performed in other names? When I read the kamitic tree of life, I understood the law of miracles.

I think I left enough information for you to research on your own. Just remember to keep an open mind. And for the ones who are conscious already, at least you know you are not crazy.

CHAPTER SIX
AFRAKAN SPIRITUALITY SCIENCE

We cannot prove Afrakan spirituality is not evil, if we can't prove how it works. What you call *spirit*, I call *energy*. What you call *spirituality*, I call *science*. That doesn't mean I don't believe in a higher power. It just means I like to explain the unknown in a plausible, tangible way.

Religion likes to keep you in the dark, so let's go to the light, shall we? By now you know words are used to keep you in the dark. Words in Afrakan spirituality brings *vibes*. Each word name brings a different energy. There is no good or evil energy. It's up to the individual person to use that energy how they choose. This is the true reason for karma, checks and balances. If you do evil, evil comes back to you.

There is no so-called God sitting on a throne in the sky. For those who practice spirituality, God is spirit energy; all around us, in us. It is up to us to tap into that energy. You have a conscious separate from your brain. We call this *Ori*, meaning *head*. The Lord of eternity speaks to you in that conscious realm. That is the word of God. Your brain also houses the third eye; pineal gland. This is the image of Haru and Ra, the all seeing eye.

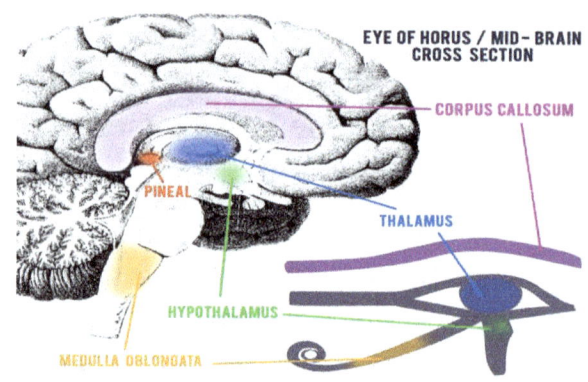

Some people use *chakra* to open their pineal gland. When that happens, people can see and sense things the naked eye can't. For example, you know when a car is going to turn before it does, seeing spirit's energy, or when someone likes you.

When you say, "I feel your vibe," this is not a figure of speech, but literally everything in the universe vibrates. Everything that vibrates gives off energy. The higher your conscious, the more open you are to vibrations (spirit's energy).

You are divine because you have the breath spirit of the Lord in you, so you judge yourself daily. The heart holds memories. This is a scientific proven fact, not a figure of speech. Your lips may say one thing, but your heart convicts you every time. In Ta Mari, your heart is weighed on a scale against the feather of Ma'at.

FROM RELIGION TO CONSCIOUSNESS

What some call *heaven*, others call *the celestial realm*. I like to call it the *ancestral realm*, because our ancestors watch over us, and we meet them in that place when we transcend. When you transcend, your spirit energy does not die, it transcends from one place to another. Your heart will determine where it goes.

Depending on what part of the divine I tap into determines what type of miracle I can perform. Look at it this way; every part of nature has a law attached to it. There is a law of gravity, a law of aviation, a law of hydrology (water), and there is the law of celestial stars. Learn the law of that nature, and you can work with – not control it. Your children were taught this on a television show called *Avatar*. This show deals with air, water, fire, earth and metal bending.

Afrakan spirituality makes more sense to me than religion, once you understand Afrakan symbolism. The Sumerian and Ta Mari story of creation makes way more sense than the bible ever could. You learn that Eve came before Adam. You learn the law of gravity and that Afrakan people's melanin needs the sun, which is something you never learn in whitewash religion. "However a man thinks, so is he." This is the true purpose behind Kamitic. Yoga is used to pose and think like that neteru, so you become that neteru.

To think like white Jesus can do nothing for me but turn me into a house Negro coon, because white Jesus cannot relate to what a black man goes through and thinks. I can relate to Ausar, "the perfect black." I can relate to Amun, the "hiding" force in the "black melanin" universe. But I cannot relate to white Jesus. Even Spanish people have been brainwashed from saying his real name.

Now you see why it is so important to get back to our culture and leave the brainwashing European religion alone. An Afrakan proverb says, "Ignorance is the root to evil." This was also written before the bible. But the point I am trying to make is ignorance causes evil. This is why my people around the globe are in the shape we're in. We have been cut off from the spiritual knowledge of our ancestors and ourselves.

"My people are destroyed from lack of knowledge." People think it is crazy for a slave to love his or her slave master, but that is what black people are doing by loving white Jesus. He has cut you off from knowing yourself.

Spirituality deals with the individual's relationship with the great divine. Religion deals with manmade customs. Afrakan spirituality deals with the Afrakan's relationship with the great divine. Buddha, Krishna and Jesus cannot save the Afrakan mind because they do not relate to Afrakan culture. Even though they were originally black, they were changed as well. All religions are simply Afrakan spirituality in a nutshell. I encourage you to do your own research and learn the truth for yourself.

CONCLUSION

For people who believe I am attacking religion, trust I am not. This book is only half of its original content. I only offered enough information for people to think. I learned that if you just tell people they have been lied to by the ones they trust, they get bitter and angry.

Mental slavery is the worst kind of slavery, because it makes you love the lie and the slave owner. If the truth makes you free, then I hope you become free.

FROM RELIGION TO CONSCIOUSNESS

At one time, when I heard white people say Jesus is white, I would try to prove them wrong. But now I realize they are right. There was no white, blue-eyed, brown-haired white man named Jesus. Instead, he is a created white god for white people. Black people need to give them their god back. Be true to your culture and yourself, instead of defending something that was not yours in the first place.

Let no one make you feel ashamed for practicing your ancestral culture. It is your divine birth right. And it worked. It was not until we bought into whitewash religion that we were defeated as a nation of people.

Hattie gained their freedom back when they gave white people there god back. Hattie is poor because the European nations turned against them when they gained their freedom back, not because they pray to divine Afrakan names. These are more lies from white preachers.

You are an individual. Think like an individual, not like a slave.

As'e *Love: Aliyahu Amun*

ELLIOTT BURNS

ABOUT THE AUTHOR

Elliott Burns was called to preach at 17 years of age. He has been going strong for 29 years. He was an assistant pastor at the age of 21. He shepherded God's people at his own assembly for 3 years before transcending from Christianity to Consciousness. Elliott is an ordained minister. He can be contacted at *chosenbygod@msn.com*. Learn more about his ministry at *chosenbygod.vpweb.com*.

www.ingramcontent.com/pod-product-compliance
Lightning Source LLC
Chambersburg PA
CBHW070545300426
44113CB00011B/1801